Contents

Fiction

The Goat's Head Pendant

Play

Bad Luck to the Bad

Non-fiction

Buried Alive

Written by
David Grant

Illustrated by
Nelson Evergreen

Series editor **Dee Reid**

ALWAYS LEARNING

PEARSON

Before reading *The Goat's Head Pendant*

Characters

Zack

The old lady

Zack's dad

New vocabulary

ch1 p4 pendant
ch1 p4 engraved
ch2 p8 portrait
ch3 p13 shuffling

ch3 p14 rasping
ch3 p15 clamped
ch3 p15 wheezed

Introduction

Zack and his dad were staying at Hill Hall Hotel. Zack finds an old pendant in the flower bed. When he shows it to the old lady who owns the hotel, she tells him a scary story about a pendant that looked like the one he has found. When Zack goes to bed that night he puts the pendant under his pillow.

The
Goat's Head
Pendant

Chapter One

Zack and his dad arrived at Hill Hall Hotel
on Friday evening. They were on their way to a
festival. As Zack lifted the bags out of the boot,
he looked at the hotel. It seemed dark and
gloomy in the fading light.

 As they were waiting for someone to answer the door, Zack noticed something in a flower bed. He bent down and picked it up. It was covered in mud, but Zack could see that it was a pendant on a chain. He wiped away some of the mud with his thumb and saw that the pendant had a star engraved on one side. The front door of the hotel creaked open and an old lady stood in the doorway. Zack slipped the pendant into his pocket. "Welcome to Hill Hall Hotel," said the old lady. Her hair was grey and her skin was almost white.

"This is where you will sleep," she told Zack as she pushed open an old, creaking door. The room smelled dusty and damp. The light was dim and the carpet was nearly worn out.

Suddenly the old lady put her face close to Zack's and he could smell her stale breath. "Was there something you wanted to show me?" she asked. *How could she know about the pendant?* thought Zack.

"I found this in the flower bed," said Zack, pulling the pendant out of his pocket and handing it to the old lady.

She looked at the pendant closely. "I could tell you a story of a pendant like this," she said.

Zack felt the hairs on the back of his neck begin to rise.

Chapter Two

"Hundreds of years ago, a man called Charles Hill found a pendant like this one," said the old lady. "It was said the pendant brought luck to anyone who found it: good luck to the good, and bad luck to the bad. Charles Hill was a poor man but the pendant brought him good luck and soon he was rich and he used his money to build Hill Hall. But his luck didn't last long."

"Charles had a son whose name was Edward," the old lady went on. "That's Edward's portrait on the wall above the bed. Does he remind you of anyone?"

Zack's heart jumped. The portrait did remind Zack of someone. It looked just like him!

"Edward was wicked," said the old lady. "He wanted the pendant because he wanted the good luck it had brought to his father."

"So one day Edward killed his father – stabbed him through the heart and buried him under the big oak tree in the garden." The old lady pointed towards the window and then said, "Edward stole the pendant but it didn't bring him good luck. He was haunted by the ghost of his murdered father and the ghost would not rest until he had taken back the pendant."

"They say that Edward was driven mad by the haunting until, one day, he ran screaming from this house and was never seen again."

"Could this be the same pendant?" asked Zack.

"No," said the old lady. "That pendant had a goat's head engraved inside the star."

As Zack got ready for bed he thought about the old lady's story. He looked again at the pendant. It still had some mud on it. As he scraped the mud off he saw something engraved inside the star. It looked a bit like an animal's head. He put the pendant under his pillow and tried to go to sleep.

Chapter Three

Zack's eyes flew open. He didn't know if he'd
been to sleep but he was definitely awake now.
The room was in complete darkness. Zack listened
carefully. He heard a faint sound like scratching on
his door.

Then Zack heard the creaking noise of his
door being slowly opened and footsteps shuffling
towards his bed.

Zack could not see a thing but he was sure that
someone was leaning over him and there was
a strange smell of damp earth. Then there was
a movement under his pillow. It felt like a hand
feeling for something.

Zack heard a rasping whisper in his ear.

"I knew you would come back one day, Edward,"

it said. "And now I have come to take what

is mine."

Zack opened his mouth to scream but a cold hand clamped his mouth shut and no sound came out.

Long, ice-cold fingers closed around Zack's throat. Zack gasped for breath as the icy fingers tightened their grip.

"I'm not Edward, I'm Zack!" gasped Zack.

The fingers tightened further.

"I'm Zack!" he wheezed.

Then Zack felt the fingers slowly uncurl from his neck. As he lay gasping for air, Zack heard the footsteps shuffling towards the door and then he heard his door creak shut. Zack turned on the lamp and looked under his pillow. The pendant was gone! He sprang out of bed to look in the mirror. His neck had ugly red scratches where he had felt the fingers.

In the dim light he saw a trail of muddy footprints leading from his door to his bed and back again. Zack didn't sleep for the rest of the night.

Chapter Four

"You look tired," said his dad the next morning.

"I had a terrible night," said Zack.

"Really?" said the old lady.

Zack and his dad jumped. They hadn't seen her come in.

"Look," she said, pointing through the window to the garden. "Something has been digging under the oak tree. That's the tree I told you about," she said, smiling at Zack.

"She was a nice old lady," said his dad as they put their bags in the car. "I think we should come back here one day."

Zack looked at the oak tree. Underneath it was a huge mound of earth like a giant molehill. It looked like someone had dug themselves out of the ground.

"No," said Zack. "I don't ever want to come back here again."

Quiz

Text comprehension

Literal comprehension

p4 What does Zack notice on one side of the pendant?

p7 Why did the pendant not bring Edward good luck?

p16 What was the proof that Zack was not dreaming about fingers around his throat?

Inferential comprehension

p4 Why does Zack slip the pendant into his pocket?

p14 Who is speaking in a rasping whisper?

p20 Why was there a mound of earth under the oak tree?

Personal response

p6 Would you have shown the old lady the pendant?

p8 How would you feel if you saw an old portrait of someone that looked just like you?

p20 Would you tell your dad about what happened in the night?

Author's style

p4–5 How does the author make the old lady seem creepy?

p13 Zack cannot see, but with which other senses does he experience his night time visitor?

p20 What simile does the author use?

Before reading *Bad Luck to the Bad*

Characters

- **Evans** (a servant)
- Sir Charles Hill (the owner of Hill Hall)
- **Lady Isobel Hill** (his wife)
- **Edward Hill** (their son)

Setting the scene

Sir Charles, Lady Isobel and Edward are sitting at a long dining table in their huge dining room in Hill Hall. Evans, their servant, is standing by ready to serve them. Edward is angry with his father who has refused to lend him any more money.

Evans: Will you have some more turkey, Sir?

Sir Charles: No, thank you, Evans.

Edward: *(angrily)* Damn it Father, you must give me some more money. I owe thousands of pounds.

Lady Isobel: You could stop gambling. How much money have you lost this week?

Sir Charles: You could try earning some money instead of expecting me to give you more and more money.

Edward: Why should I bother to earn money? If you would give me the goat's head pendant it would bring me the good luck it has brought you. I would have money to burn!

Evans: Should I serve pudding, Mr Edward?

Edward: Be quiet Evans! I don't want pudding, I want some of the money my selfish father refuses to give me!

Lady Isobel: Please excuse Mr Edward's rudeness.

Evans: I'll get the pudding.

Edward: *(grabbing the carving knife)* I must have that pendant.

Evans: Be careful, Mr Edward. That knife is very sharp.

Edward: Shut up Evans! I will have that goat's head pendant.

Lady Isobel: Sit down, Edward.

Sir Charles: Put the knife down, Edward.

Edward: Give me the pendant now!

Sir Charles: The goat's head pendant will stay around my neck. Just as it has done for the last twenty years. You will have it when I die just as you will have everything when I die.

Edward: And how long will I have to wait until you die?

Lady Isobel: What a cruel thing to say!

Edward: I must have the pendant now!

Sir Charles: How old was my father when he died, Evans?

Evans: Let me think, Sir. He must have been 93 years old.

Sir Charles: So you just have to wait another twenty years and you will be a very rich man.

Edward: I will not wait twenty years! I will kill you now and have the pendant.

Edward stabs his father.

Lady Isobel: What have you done? You've stabbed your own father! Surely you know that the goat's head brings good luck to the good and bad luck to the bad. What kind of luck do you think you will have now?

Evans: Let me try to stop the bleeding.

Sir Charles: Get a doctor. I'm dying.

Evans: Yes, Sir. Right away, Sir.

Edward: Evans?

Evans: Sir?

Edward: Don't bother with a doctor. Just get a spade and dig a hole under the oak tree.

Evans: I don't understand, Sir. You want me to dig a hole? Why?

Edward: So I can bury this selfish old man.

Lady Isobel: Ignore him, Evans. Get a doctor at once. Edward, how could you be so cruel to your father who has always given you money to pay off your debts.

Sir Charles: *(gasping for breath)* I warn you, Edward. If I die, you must bury that pendant with me.

Edward: *(laughing)* And miss out on all the money it could bring me? Never!

Sir Charles: If that pendant is not buried with me, I will come back from the dead and haunt you until your dying day!

As Sir Charles dies, Edward's laugh gets louder and louder.

Quiz

Text comprehension

p23 How has Edward wasted the family money?
p27 Why will Edward not have good luck with the pendant?
p29 What threat does Sir Charles make?

Vocabulary

p24 Find a word meaning 'mean'.
p24 Find a phrase meaning 'won't let me have'.
p28 Find a word meaning 'pay no attention to'.

Before reading Buried Alive!

Find out about

- what people did to avoid being buried alive.

New vocabulary

p33 coma

p33 unconscious

p34 crowbars

p34 inventors

p36 raised

p37 magician

Introduction

One thing that most people would be scared of is being buried alive and a few hundred years ago that was a real risk. Doctors sometimes thought patients were dead when they were not and there were stories of people sitting up in their coffins at the funeral service. So inventors made safety coffins so that if someone was buried alive they could contact people above ground.

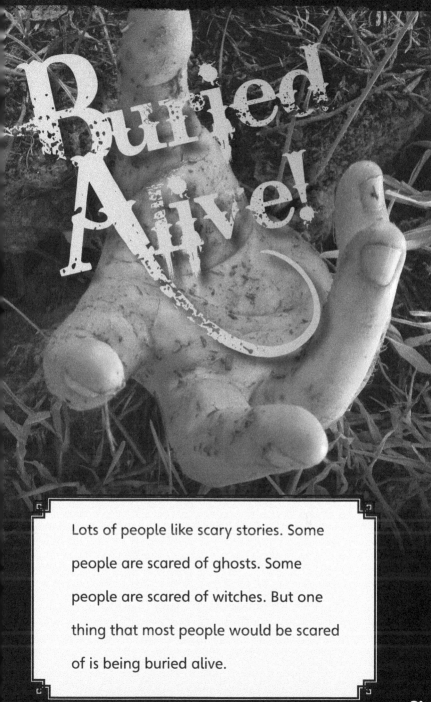

Buried Alive!

Lots of people like scary stories. Some people are scared of ghosts. Some people are scared of witches. But one thing that most people would be scared of is being buried alive.

Dodgy Doctors

A few hundred years ago, doctors were not so good at deciding if a patient was dead or not. If a patient was not moving and the doctor could not find their heartbeat, the doctor decided they were dead. There are stories of bodies in coffins waiting to be buried and the body sitting up and getting out of the coffin! The doctor had made a mistake – the patient hadn't died at all!

So people were scared that they might be buried in the ground when really they were just in a coma or unconscious. They were scared they might wake up too late and find themselves buried alive.

Safety Coffin

Some people asked to be buried with crowbars and spades so they could open the coffin, dig their way out and escape if they were buried alive. Inventors realised they could make lots of money from people's fear of being buried alive. They decided to make safety coffins.

One type of safety coffin placed a rope in the dead person's hand. The top of the rope was connected to a bell which was above the ground. If the person in the coffin moved at all, the bell would ring and people would dig up the coffin and the person could escape.

Another type of safety coffin had an air tube. One end of the tube was placed inside the coffin. The tube went up from the coffin to the ground above, so if you woke up and you were buried alive you could breathe and call for help. One inventor tested his safety coffin by being buried alive in it. He spent a few hours underground and he even had a meal of soup and sausages sent down the air tube!

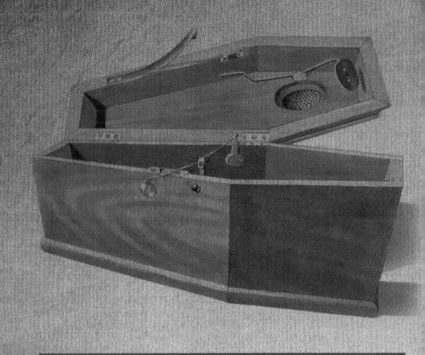

Another type of safety coffin had a flag. If the person in the coffin moved at all, a flag above the ground would be raised and people would dig up the coffin. There are no records of any lives being saved by a safety coffin, but hundreds of people bought safety coffins because they were so scared of being buried alive.

Escape!

In 1917, there was a magician called Harry Houdini. He was famous for escaping from handcuffs and ropes. He decided to show that he could escape being buried alive. He was buried in a hole two metres underground. Houdini dug his way out but when he reached the top he fainted and he nearly died.

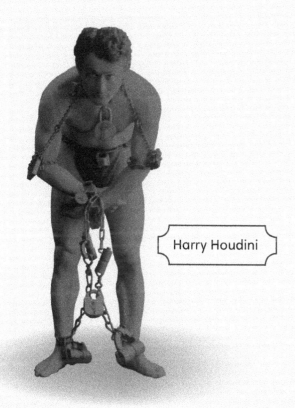

Harry Houdini

In 1999, a magician called David Blaine spent seven days buried in a plastic coffin. He survived by drinking three spoonfuls of water a day. Luckily, there's no chance of anyone being buried alive today. Unless they are a magician who wants to be buried alive for a trick!

Quiz

Literal comprehension
p32 What mistake did some doctors make?
p34 Why did some people ask to be buried with a spade?
p36 How did the safety coffin with the flag work?

Inferential comprehension
p34 In what ways were the inventors clever?
p35 Why did the inventor ask to be buried alive in his own safety coffin?
p38 Why was David Blaine's coffin made of plastic?

Personal response
- How would you feel if a person in a coffin sat up during the funeral service?
- Do you think the safety features in coffins would really work? Why?
- What do you think about David Blaine's trick?

Non-fiction features

p35 How could you divide the information about the safety coffin with an air tube into three bullet points?
p35 Think of a subheading for this page.
p38 Think of a subheading for this page.

Published by Pearson Education Limited, Edinburgh Gate, Harlow, Essex, CM20 2JE.

www.pearsonschoolsandfecolleges.co.uk

Text © Pearson Education Limited 2012

Edited by Bethan Phillips
Designed by Tony Richardson and Siu Hang Wong
Original illustrations © Pearson Education Limited 2012
Illustrated by Nelson Evergreen
Cover design by Siu Hang Wong
Picture research by Melissa Allison
Cover illustration © Pearson Education Limited 2012

The right of David Grant to be identified as author of this work has been asserted by him in accordance with the Copyright, Designs and Patents Act 1988.

First published 2012

2024
18

British Library Cataloguing in Publication Data
A catalogue record for this book is available from the British Library

ISBN 978 0 435 07154 7

Printed in Great Britain by Ashford Colour Press Ltd.

Acknowledgements
The author and publisher would like to thank the following individuals and organisations for permission to reproduce photographs:

(Key: b-bottom; c-centre; l-left; r-right; t-top)

Corbis: National Archives 36; Getty Images: Hulton Archive 1, 35, Liaison Agency / Jeff Christensen 38, Superstock 32-33; iStockphoto: spxChrome 31; Rex Features: Everett Collection 37; Shutterstock.com: Jake Rennaker 34

Cover images: Back: iStockphoto: spxChrome

All other images © Pearson Education

Every effort has been made to contact copyright holders of material reproduced in this book. Any omissions will be rectified in subsequent printings if notice is given to the publishers.